Lauren,
Thanks for bringing light and
laughter to WVW16!
May your cup runneth over!

Kat Simmons

Single Feather Publishing

Kat's Daily Cups

A Collection of Stories about
Children, Animals & Inspiration

Written by Kat Simmons

Illustrated by Emma Stamper

Dedication

This book is dedicated to my children, Jonathan Maclain and Emma Kate Stamper. I love you both deeply and forever. Please remember to eat your greens.

Photograph by Allison Ramsey

Kat's Daily Cups

TABLE OF CONTENTS

TITLE		PAGE
Introduction		11
PART I.	**PARENTING**	15
Chapter 1.	A Daily Cup of Emma's Shoes	16
Chapter 2.	A Daily Cup of Art	20
Chapter 3.	A Daily Cup of Root Beer	24
Chapter 4.	A Daily Cup of The Little Blue Sock	28
Chapter 5.	A Daily Cup of Creative Parenting	32
Chapter 6.	A Daily Cup of Children	38
PART II.	**ANIMALS**	43
Chapter 7.	A Daily Cup of Stray Dogs	44
Chapter 8.	A Daily Cup of Pugs	50
Chapter 9.	A Daily Cup of Moths	54
Chapter 10.	A Daily Cup of the Sitting Horse	60
PART III.	**RELATIONSHIPS**	65
Chapter 11.	A Daily Cup of Waves	66
Chapter 12.	A Daily Cup of Passion	70
Chapter 13.	A Daily Cup of Projection	76
Chapter 14.	A Daily Cup of Why	82

PART IV.   **HOLIDAYS**   87

Chapter 15.   A Daily Cup of Christmas Tradition   88

Chapter 16.   A Daily Cup of Reindeer   94

Chapter 17.   A Daily Cup of Christmas Expectations   98

Chapter 18.   A Daily Cup of Really Good Coffee   102

PART V.   **LIFE & DEATH**   105

Chapter 19.   A Daily Cup of Dragonflies   106

Chapter 20.   A Daily Cup of Contemplation   110

Chapter 21.   A Daily Cup of White Mice   114

Chapter 22.   A Daily Cup of L'Air Du Temps   122

Chapter 23.   A Daily Cup of Letting Go of Laughter   126

PART VI.   **AWAKENINGS**   131

Chapter 24.   A Daily Cup of Perfection   132

Chapter 25.   A Daily Cup of Ego   136

Chapter 26.   A Daily Cup of Fortune Cookies   140

Chapter 27.   A Daily Cup of Toilets   144

Chapter 28.   A Daily Cup of Empathy   148

Chapter 29.   A Daily Cup of Activism   152

Chapter 30.   A Daily Cup of Seven Minutes   156

BONUS.   What is in your Daily Cup?   160

ACKNOWLEDGMENTS   171

ABOUT THE AUTHOR   175

Introduction

"The writer writes not because he is educated but because he is driven by the need to communicate. Behind the need to communicate is the need to share. Behind the need to share is the need to be understood." - Leo Rosten

When my son was little, he once said, "Mommy, I think I know why dogs go round and round in circles before they lay down at night."

"Why?" I asked.

"Because they are making a little invisible fence around them to protect them while they sleep," he said.

That visual popped into my head as I sat down to write this. I feel like one of those dogs before bedtime right now. Sitting down to write about myself is far harder than anything else I wrote in this book.

These stories wrote themselves really, and I just reported them to the best of my ability. I was moved in some way before writing each of them. When I feel the need to write, it is not a choice. I am driven to catch the feelings and turn them into words before they vanish. Writing has been therapy for me for a very long time. It is a way to get what's going on inside of me out, and hopefully my words, that are just symbols for the feelings, will resonate and touch you as well. My need to connect and share is what drives me.

The idea for these stories started one day after what could have been an untimely demise for me. You will read about it in the "A Daily Cup of Reindeer" story; it was my first one.

After I stopped shaking and composed myself, I began to laugh hysterically, and thought my life was full of crazy stories that I needed to share. That day was the beginning of my "Daily Cup of Chaos" series. I was and am a single mother, and I really needed someone to talk to. I took the hard times, and spun them into laughter, because that is the gift of being a comedian. I will celebrate thirty years in the comedy world on January 9, 2017. Every comic remembers their first time on stage. Comedy will teach you to look at life differently. One person's nightmare is five new minutes on stage for me. Miracles are often just a shift in perception.

However, being a believer in metaphysics and manifesting that which I focus on, I decided I did not want to be locked into having daily chaos in my life for the sake of writing, and opened myself to all life's possibilities. Not all my stories are funny, as you will see. Life is not always funny; it is messy, rich and wonderful, but loss and sadness are unavoidable when you also feel love.

I began journaling in my early twenties, and putting pen to paper was my salvation. It was a place I could always go, and share my feelings without fearing red marks from teachers, or being judged for being "too sensitive." People say that like it is a bad thing, but at the end of the day, despite the pain that sometimes comes with being an empath, I am happy that is who I grew up to be.

I encourage you to use my book and make it your own. I hope it will be a place for you to be entertained, laugh, cry, and be inspired. I have always said, that if I could make people laugh and cry at the same time, my mission was accomplished. Feelings are there to be expressed, so have at it. Use this book to write your own experiences and feelings as well. What is in your Daily Cup today?

In addition to using this book to record your own stories, it is also a place to come play. We all need to play more. In fact, I think we should all keep our swing sets; I still have ours. Okay, mostly because I sun dry laundry on it, and I don't have the heart to kick the wasps out, but it is a good reminder of times gone by. Coloring is playing, too, and it is a way to unplug, create, and relax. Please fill your cup with your own unique colors, creations, and memories. Let this book become your book as well.

Thank you for buying "Kat's Daily Cups." Please stay tuned for my second book, as my cup runneth over for sure. It has been my greatest joy to share some of my life and experiences with you. I would love to hear how this book may have inspired you to write your own stories, as well as coloring your own artistic creations. Please feel free to share them with me on Facebook, Twitter, and Instagram.

Kat Simmons

www.KatSimmons.com

Facebook Kat-Simmons Entertainer

https://twitter.com/katsimmonscomic

https://www.instagram.com/katlaffs/

Welcome to Kat's Daily Cups!

PART I. PARENTING

Chapter One

A Daily Cup of Emma's Shoes

A pair of tiny, black patent leather shoes remained on the shelf long after all the other hand me downs found their way to other little girls. My sister had three daughters before me and passed down all her favorite treasures. They became a shrine of hope for the little girl I might have one day. Sadly, I lost a baby three years after I had Jon. I was almost three months pregnant, and it was more devastating than I could have imagined. We placed an angel in my front garden to memorialize the sweet one I did not get to meet.

Two years passed and it began to look like there was not going to be another baby in my life. Little by little, I began to let go of all those precious pink and lacey clothes, but I could not part with those shoes. Many times I would retrieve them from the giveaway bag, and put them back on the shelf where I would visualize a little girl's pudgy feet in them one day. They were a symbol of hope for me. They were a promise I kept to both of us.

Three years later, I found out I was pregnant, despite the doctors telling me my chances were not good. They also told me a woman of my age "should really think about it." I chose not to listen to them. I got pregnant the first time we made a decision to try again after so long. No longer did I feel a deep sadness and loss, almost a tug from the other side when I meditated. I was always sure it was the presence of the baby I lost. It had now been replaced by a warmth and a knowing. I really believe Emma was waiting to come back to me when the time was better.

Emma Kate was born the week before my 43rd birthday, on February 3rd. She was perfect in every way. After she was born, they placed her in my hands to hold. I kept holding her until I left the hospital the next day. They encouraged me to put her in the bassinet, but I declined. I knew she would be my last baby. I also knew a day would come when I would have to let go, but until then, I was going to hold her. When she breathed, she made this sweet little sound, almost like a puppy. The nurses could not really figure it out, and then we all just decided it was audible bliss.

When she was about a year and a half old, she was out in the garden playing naked, as she usually was. She went over to the statue of the angel; its wings now overgrown with fragrant honeysuckle, and hugged it like it was an old friend. Maybe it was?

When I took Emma and my son, Jon, in for their first professional portrait, I could not wait to put those shoes on her. It would be proof that all that manifesting worked. Well, I could not fit those adorable, pudgy feet into those shoes, but they are in the picture next to her dimpled feet.

Chapter Two

A Daily Cup of Art

My daughter came out of the womb with an energy and determination that let me know right away that she was going to be very independent.

When she was a toddler, I used to lay her clothes out in the morning, but I always gave her several choices to pick from. I thought all my choices were great, but she had other ideas. One morning during our usual struggle, she placed her hands on her little hips and looked up at me, and said indignantly, "You know, Mommy, everyone has their own certain ways." There was something about that statement that just allowed me to surrender, because it was just so true.

I remember when we would drop my son, Jon, off in morning and she would cry and cry, "I want to go to school, I want to go to school!"

One day, I was on the edge of losing it, so I drove her to a Montessori school. I arrived exasperated and said, "We are not enrolled here, but can we please come in?" I just needed to let her feel like she was in school, too. I later found a preschool that would take her at the tender age of 22 months. She had to be potty trained but she had that handled as soon as she could walk. It felt so odd leaving my baby there for a few hours twice a week, but I got used to it. Right about the time I was really in the groove, she decided it was not fun anymore and did not go back to preschool until she was four.

Emma was one of the most creative children I have ever seen. If she did not have it, she would make it. She had an entire wardrobe and accessories for her dolls made out of paper. She hung them up on a white board with tiny pieces of tape.

One day, at the age of three, she made some artwork and announced, "I am going to go sale these."

At first I told her, "No, you cannot just go out there by yourself door-to-door and try to sell your drawings." But then a voice came from somewhere deep inside that said, "Don't squash her dream. If she thinks she can, let her." She packed up her creations and headed off under my watchful eye. Emma, being Emma, would not allow me to come along. I was the only Mom that did not get to walk their child into kindergarten on the first day. So I hid behind the column on the front porch and watched her go to three different homes. I was not sure she could even reach the doorbell. She came home with a big smile and whopping $1.25 in her little brown drawstring coin purse. I have kept that money in there for her all these years. I will never forget the lesson that the little girl with her "own certain ways" taught me that day and will continue to teach me for the rest of my days.

It is no surprise to me that on the day before my daughter turns 17, she will also be the illustrator for my first book. She and I have not always seen eye to eye, but this book will be a labor of love for us and something for both my children to look back on in years to come.

Chapter Three

A Daily Cup of Root Beer

"Hurry up, you'll be late," is my usual mantra about 8:55 am every morning as I am rounding my daughter up for school.

Yesterday, when I pulled into the circular drop off driveway, or the "horseshoe of insanity," as I call it, the electric van door seemed to be jammed. I repeatedly pushed the door to no avail. I immediately thought of the huge bill for fixing what would surely be an extensive electrical problem.

Just after she hurdled over the front seat to escape the van, the door reluctantly opened with a strange creaking sound. I pushed the button a time or two more, just to make sure it was indeed working. The door continued to open, and the horrible sound accompanied it every time.

Then, I saw IT: the paper cup from our last fast food experience. I knew it had been nearly full when she put it in the cup holder. When I picked it up, it was almost empty, and as much as I wished it had evaporated, I knew in my gut where it had gone.

My door did not have an electrical problem, but more of an adhesive problem. In fact, it had been sealed shut with root beer. It created a little river and traveled down into the side pocket with happy meal toys, mismatched mittens, and some other things I am afraid I did not even recognize. Everything was shellacked together like a soda pop mosaic.

This reminded me of another soda incident when my son dropped a can of ginger ale on the floor and for reasons unknown, it got a puncture in it, and spun around like a Fourth of July effervescent firecracker, spraying the entire kitchen with its contents. I did not realize at the time how much territory it covered. To this day, when I go to open certain cupboards, I am met with resistance, and there is always that same sticky sound as I break the seal. I think in that moment, "I really need to get some hot, soapy water and clean this."

Four years have passed since then, and I have pretended I had the cupboards varnished instead. So, if you need something glued, check your cupboards for soda first. It can be quite handy.

Chapter Four

A Daily Cup of The Little Blue Sock

My son's drawer was jammed, I am sure due to the "creative" way he puts his clothes away. After years of this technique, the rollers have now jumped the track and the drawer hangs precariously from the track.

The other day, I finally resigned myself to the fact that he was not going to take it out and investigate the problem, but just shove it in harder. Once I removed the drawer, I looked down at the floor to find a tiny blue sock. At first I thought it must have been my daughter's sock from when she was younger, but soon realized to my sadness, that it was his, and that time had just flown by. We moved into this house when he was only five, and he is now teenager. I inspected it, trying to remember how it looked on his foot. I wondered where the mate was, and then soon realized it must be with the other hundred or so missing socks that have vanished from this house. Really, how can that even be mathematically possible? They must be with all the missing Tupperware lids.

I washed that little sock, I am not sure why, and now I have one more clean sock without a mate. However, this sock is different. It does not annoy me. It wasn't left in the car, under the bed, by the X-Box, wadded up and stuffed behind the TV, or out on the lawn. I recently found some socks that had been taken off while wet, rolled up in a ball, and left outside. They barely resembled socks, after being out in the elements for a season or two.

This little sock is a reminder to me, of how fast my son is growing up, and the wonderful person he is becoming. I know that all too soon, he will be gone, and I will long for the days when I saw his dirty, little mismatched socks all over my house. I will wish I could yell out from the other room, "Jon, how many times have I told you to pick up these socks?" But, he will not be here to answer. Oh sure, there may eventually be order here again, but how fun will that be? My son may be missing socks, but what he lacks in socks, he makes up for in character and heart.

Chapter Five

A Daily Cup of Creative Parenting

There is that day, you know the one, when you hit that wall of frustration with your kids and you have to find a better way. Today is that day.

I refuse to be outsmarted or manipulated by children anymore. A war of creativity has been declared; let the games begin. After all, I am older and wiser, am I not?

I have survived 24 years as a stand up comic, working seedy gigs with shady people, and I have managed to keep doing the thing I love, while I am still a stay-at-home mom. That took some doing, so why can't I make my kids do what I want? How can this be so challenging?

It is a daily battle, and I know the outcome; I will be red-faced and frustrated as they shrug off their crazy mother. So, how do I this differently?

Today, my 17-year-old son stood right in front of me and emptied the sand from his shoes onto my carpet. Now I realize my carpet most likely has its own life cycle by now, but still, really, right in front of me? It was like he just could not differentiate between the outdoors and my living room. Then he asked for me to find him socks that match, and I took great pleasure in saying, "I do not want to deprive you of a chance to be responsible." He grumbled as he walked away, and I felt much better for not yelling, "Find it yourself! I am not the maid, are your arms broken?"

His once white socks take up a lot of space in my head. It is mathematically impossible to have as many strays as we do here. No, really, you have no idea how many unmatched socks he has. *Why couldn't I be one of those really together moms who always buys the same socks, so there are never any mismatches?* I will tell you why.

For one, I could never remember where I bought the previous ones or what brand they were; he is lucky I remember to buy them at all. All I know, is that I am always hopeful when I bring home that little hygienic bag, stuffed with all those white as the driven snow socks. So, when he asks *me* to find him socks, I get to release a little resentment for all the socks I have ever seen scattered all over the house, when I refuse to help him. Really, if he took even 1% of the time he spends watching motocross or men eating gigantic portions of food on You Tube, and matched his socks that are currently overflowing out of his cubby, (you know those little spaces in closets for organizing) ha, what a joke that is; he would have enough socks to last until he was growing hair out of his ears. So, today when he gets home, he will be vacuuming the entire house before he does any surfing on You Tube.

As soon as he walks out the door in the morning, my 12-year-old daughter wakes up to some screeching song on her cell phone that she begged me for. I finally caved, under the pretense of "at least I will know where she is after school." This phone is now my enemy. I wonder who she is talking to, and why? She was texting while doing homework last night, and I told her to stop it. She proudly told me she was "multi-tasking," as though she was some student of the new age. I cannot shelter her from everything, but I still want to. I am not ready to have my baby splitting off from me, but she is.

Fake fingernails have become her latest obsession. Am I a bad mom because I let her buy them with her own money? I remember being 12 and making fake fingernails out of clay and paper, and holding my hands upside down in the bathtub while watching the droplets of water hang from the tips of my nails, making them look longer, sexier, better. Yes, I have very clear memories of how much I wanted pretty nails, but my parents would not even allow me to wear nail polish at that age. As she waved her pretty little hands (the ones that just yesterday had dimples on them), in front of me this morning, clearly feeling better about herself than if she were just herself. I felt sad but also secretly coveted those nails. I cannot contain or squash this budding young woman, but I absolutely can teach her how to be okay as is. Is that possible? Am I an idealist here? I cringe thinking about her always wanting something outside of herself to make her happy.

They all have little "boyfriends" at school, and I am sure it is harmless, but I fear for what is yet to come. We argue a lot these days, and I am digging down deep to get creative. When I feel myself pushed up against that familiar wall, and I want to get bigger than her with my emotion, I will do my best to say, "I love you too much to fight with you."

I have been driving my kids to school for nearly 13 years, and in less than two months that part of our lives will be over. Our drive can either be the 6 minutes of shame drive, or one of love and listening. I am committed to make it the latter. It is all going so fast now, and I have flashbacks of all the parents who looked at me with envy when my kids were little while saying, "Appreciate it, they grow so fast." Whoever those people were, they were right. I feel like I want to appreciate, sculpt and be present for all the moments yet to come. *Have I taught them enough, did I tell them to dry between their toes, or the right way to floss, or to pray or meditate?*

As I walked out of the house this morning, looking at the vitamins my son leaves behind every morning, the dirty white sock in the hall, the fake fingernails and all the paraphernalia that goes with them, all over my counter, the overweight pug that I

36

implore my son to walk every day, the clutter on the bulletin board from all the things they have accomplished, I get in my car on this sunny, spring morning, vow to be more detached, and pick my battles. I realize I cannot control it all, but I can change my attitude. And just for today, I did! I will give it a go tomorrow, too!

Chapter Six

A Daily Cup of Children

My children, now 17 and 12, are still sleeping. I love this quiet time in the morning to have my daily cup of coffee and hope my face does not look too obvious when they come in and interrupt it. There is something about having my daily cup of coffee in the silence that serves as my morning meditation. Sure, it would be better if I was really meditating, but at least I am being quiet.

Summers are changing around here. For the first time, my kids are both so busy with their collective group of friends that I no longer have to be the entertainment director. Now I am just the chauffeur and financier. Yesterday, for the first time, I allowed my daughter to pal around the subdivision with her buddies and yes, there were some boys. I thought back on all the times I have seen large groups of kids walking in the neighborhood, and silently judged, wondering where their parents were. Well, now it is my daughter out in a pack of kids. I have learned that anything I have ever judged has come to pass for me too.

My son went up to Tahoe with a bunch of his teenage buddies, and I am sure bikinis were involved, and my daughter was trolling along in the suburbs. The day struck me profoundly, as I really understood how fast it is all going. I breathed a huge sigh of relief when they were both back home under my roof and under my energetic wings.

I was exhausted from wondering where each one was all day, and the constant cell phone check-ins: did they use sunscreen, did they drink water, did they eat anything with a living enzyme?

Mothering is hard work and at some point you just hope that all that guidance turns into self-directed action on their part.

Today I just hope maybe they will stay home, but I doubt it. It is summer, and it is time to "hang out." This is what they do now instead of play.

I think I will have time for one more cup of coffee before they wake up.

PART II. ANIMALS

Chapter Seven

A Daily Cup of Stray Dogs

I looked out the window while having dinner at a friend's house to see a dog that looked displaced. He was golden and looked like he might be part lab with some hound mix. My friend assured me he must live close by, but I have an uncanny knack for reading animals and could see he was out of sorts. I approached him carefully to check for tags, but as usual, not even a collar.

I opened my car door to put my child in and the dog leapt in right past him, then planted himself on the seat like he had done it a hundred times before. He would not get out of the car. Now what was I supposed to do, kick him out only to have him watch us drive away into the dark of night? I brought him home with me, knowing I would take him to the shelter the next day. However, on the way home it became apparent to me that he had a hacking cough, so I called my girlfriend and asked her to keep my little dog overnight until I got him placed. The next morning, I took him to the vet to find that he had kennel cough and no one would take him. I could not bring my dog home or he would get it, so the forced bonding began. I made signs, put ads in the paper, and was sure someone would claim him. No one called. I had to go on a vacation that weekend, so he had to come since he was still contagious. He slept next to my bed and was a perfect dog the entire time. We decided to call him Barkley.

We returned from vacation and had to leave him in the backyard alone for the first time. When we got home, it looked as if someone had tried to break in. The screens were torn and bent, the door was destroyed, and his chest was soaking wet with his own saliva from nervously licking and chewing at the sliding glass door. I was shocked that his behavior had changed so much. I came to realize that as long as he could see me he was the perfect dog, but if I left his side he experienced severe separation anxiety. Having my own issues with abandonment, my empathy was deep, yet I now felt like a prisoner.

The next time I had to go out he dug out under the fence. I came home and he was gone. As I told my crying son that Barkley had made a choice to leave us I heard barking at the front door. He was home; he had not left us, but was merely looking for me. His greetings were long and exuberant.

I took him to the shelter when he recovered from the cough, hoping he would find a new home. I sponsored his adoption so that perhaps it would entice someone to adopt an older dog with issues. I called every day to ask if he had been placed but the answer was always the same. One day my husband came home and said, "Just go get the dog, we will make it work." I knew he was really against another dog, especially a disturbed one, but he could not stand looking at me thinking about him. Other than giving birth to my children, this may have been one of the happiest days of my life. I sped off to the shelter to get him. When they brought him out through the door he saw me, and they could not hold him back. Within seconds I had an eighty-pound dog in my lap. My son Jonathan was jubilant, and it seemed like this would be a happy ending for all of us.

Well, within weeks my backyard looked like a prison from trying to keep this dog in there. I had concrete poured under both gates now, a fenced kennel that he chewed right through, and finally electric fencing installed.

I had finally had it and called the shelter. I told them that when I left that day he would be at large stalking me, and for them to just pick him up. I couldn't take it anymore. They told me if they did pick him up and he did get euthanized, that I would have to sign a paper. I was so distraught and was not present for my family and felt nuts. I had to do what was best for the rest of us at this point; after all I am a good mother, right? I told him good-bye that day, knowing he would escape as always. I told him if he needed to go, then go, all his needs were met with us even if he could not see it. My stomach ached visualizing what must be going on in my absence. I came home that afternoon prepared for the sadness that would surely greet me. As I walked into the house I was so surprised to see his smiling face and wagging tail at the glass door. I inspected the back yard to find not even the smallest hole or sign of damage. It appeared that he had made a decision not to leave that day, and he never tried to escape again.

I hired a trainer to come work with him, as he thought he was the boss of the house and often growled and even snapped once at my husband. My son was only four and I feared that Barkley would bite him if he woke him up or got too close to his food. Little by little we re-educated Barkley and with each new lesson he seemed to feel safer, as did we. He was now really a part of the family and even loved my other little dog. He would sneak up on the bed at night and after a while I did not make him get down. We just pretended to not notice.

I found out I was pregnant after we had had him for a year. The fear of how he would act with a baby terrified me. My son was now old enough to know better than to climb on his back or go near his food dish, but a baby would be different. I could not face having to get rid of him again after all we had been through.

In my eighth month of pregnancy, I found out that Barkley had a very rare and aggressive form of cancer. It was already in his lymph glands, so surgery was out of the question. The vet gave him a month at best. I wondered if he would even make it until Emma was born. We decided to give him the very best quality of life we could until he left us. I ordered magic herbs and made special food hoping that perhaps a miracle would occur, but the tumor only got bigger, right along with my stomach.

The night I went into labor it was Barkley, not my husband, who stayed up with me and counted contractions with his tail. He did not leave my side until I went to the hospital. When I returned home with my beautiful daughter in her car seat I was apprehensive about how he would react. I let him smell her and get used to her a little at a time. He was so happy and followed her around everywhere. He slept next to her crib or door and never took his eyes off her. I felt safe enough a few days later to put her down on the floor to take a sunbath. I watched carefully to make sure he did not step on her or get rough. Within moments he laid down too, and put his head right next to hers as if to say, "You see, I never would have hurt her." From that time on, that was his baby. The other animals paid little attention to her, but he seemed to be her guardian angel.

Emma got to have her special friend dote over her for the next two months. He had already lived much longer than they expected, and we felt blessed to have him meet the new baby that we so feared he may hurt. The vet came to our home and Barkley was freed from his pain in front of a roaring fire on a cold winter day while lying in my arms. Emma bounced happily next to him in her baby seat, and this time she got to be there for him, the same way he had been there for her during my labor and that morning in the sun.

Chapter Eight

A Daily Cup of Pugs

My son said something last night that really cracked me up. His dog, Polly the Pug, turns around and around in circles before she lies down with him for the night.

"I think I know why dogs do that. It is because they are making a little invisible fence around them to protect them at night," he said.

Well, the other two dogs just sleep on my head, so I guess they think I'll protect them.

Polly is special, especially to my son Jonathan. I was not interested in getting a Pug, but he was convinced that Pug was the only kind of dog for him. Most boys want a big dog, a Labrador or Golden Retriever, but my son wanted a smashed face, no nose, snoring, snotting, fungus producing dog. She has an eating disorder too, and eats toilet paper, fuzz, hairballs, tacks, pencils, toys . . . well, basically anything that has a shape. She has a hard time breathing as well, which is torture for me. We even had that operation to make her nostrils bigger and some fatty tissue removed from the back of her throat to help her breathe and not snore as much.

When I was married this was a sore subject for me, as I was sleep deprived for eleven years. I am now addicted to ear plugs and cannot sleep without them. If I don't have them in I think I can actually hear the air. Just when I am finally catching up on my sleep since my divorce, Polly arrives and takes his place.

Once she nearly choked to death on a "Greenie Bone." I was hysterical, trying to give her the Heimlich maneuver and reaching down her throat only to be bitten, because I am sure she thought I was trying to kill her. I went to my neighbor's door, sobbing and bleeding, and begged them to call 911. They would not call, but they did reach a vet and off I sped at 9:00 pm. She was barely breathing, as she lay motionless in my lap, those big, bulgy eyes looking up at me. I was breathing through her nose, trying to keep enough oxygen in her to prevent brain damage although I suspect she may have come to us with some to begin with.

Once I got to the vet's office I pounded on the side door and handed her nearly lifeless body to the assistant and prayed she would make it. The vet came out moments later and my heart stopped.

"You got here just in time," the vet said.

My body relaxed for the first time since this ordeal started. I asked him how much more time she had to live, and he replied, "About a minute."

She is lying next to me now like always as I type, and neither one of those operations helped her breathe any better. So she is snoring away, which is now music to my ears and always will be.

By the way, my ex-husband had that surgery after we divorced but I will never know if it worked.

Chapter Nine

A Daily Cup of Moths

Animals come to me in groups at different times in my life, for different lessons. This summer is all about moths. Sadly, I seem to have some kind of life cycle, science project happening in my house right now. I am invaded by these small gray moths that I suspect came in through the pantry. They just seem to appear and I find them floating in the dog water, where I promptly scoop them out and put them outside to dry off. I am doomed because I cannot kill them, so I am either a Buddhist or neurotic. I would rather they go somewhere else, but I cannot just wipe them out of my home. I did this dance for years with sugar ants and people would exclaim, "You have ants!" with a bit of fear in their voice.

I would respond, "Yes we do, please be careful not to step on them." They have finally moved on and for that I am most grateful.

Yesterday when I went into the garage I heard this sound that resembled a rattlesnake. I was hoping I would not have to negotiate that kind of encounter before my first cup of coffee. Upon further investigation I realized it was a huge moth that was stuck inside the light fixture. I dug the ladder out and looked over the top, clearly seeing that if it got in, it could get out. However, the moth seemed to have missed this information and just continued to frantically beat its wings against the plastic, making a noise similar to the one I remember as a kid when we would put cards in our bike spokes to make our ride sound cool. I guess it was like our first muffler.

Well, I cannot just walk away from this moth and let him get burned from the light when I open the garage door, or let him just flutter himself to death. So I retrieved a ladder and a Phillips head screwdriver, and went to work freeing this creature. I felt like the rescue workers that rescued baby Jessica from that well years ago. I told him to just hang on a bit longer as my aging eyes adjusted to the small slits on the screws, finally making contact with them and removing the cover, which fell to the floor along with the moth. I thought now I had surely killed him in an attempt to save him.

I stooped down to pick up this mammoth of a moth and saw his wings were all tattered and nearly translucent. My heart sank, as I questioned, what kind of a life he would have now? I cursed myself, thinking I had added to his suffering by freeing him and had interfered with his life and karma. I heard my parents' voices telling me, "Kat, you can't save the world." I wondered why I could not just walk by and let the moth be? Why couldn't I just tough love this guy? Is something wrong with me or right with me? I understand that suffering is a part of life and at this very moment living things all over the planet are suffering. I hold space for all of them and send out a vision of wellbeing every day.

I walked around to my front garden and thought I would just put him near the honeysuckle vine. I gently placed him down, and to my amazement he flew back to my shoulder. We repeated this three more times, and I began to have hope for this little guy. Was he flying back to me because I looked like a light with my red hair, just because I was close, or because he felt safe? Well, I will never know the answer to that, but the fourth time I put him back he flew again with more speed and strength and bypassed me, opting for the blue of the sky instead. I was amazed and so relieved as I really thought he was grounded by the way his wings looked. If he had been a person with a serious medical condition, a doctor might have told him he would never fly again or he was terminal. I am glad he did not know this, and despite all odds took flight like a champion. That magic fairy dust that is on their wings is so powerful and so fragile, all at the same time.

We all have some of that on us, and sometimes it gets worn off. We get beat up and some of us listen to others about what we can and cannot do. I for one will always remember that moth as he flew away on a crisp fall morning. I know for me, I had done the right thing, and thought, "No, I cannot save the world, just the things in front of me."

Chapter Ten

A Daily Cup of the Sitting Horse

The dust was the first thing that caught my attention that warm August day. Through the veil, lit by the late afternoon sun, I saw him for the first time. The vaquero was trying to break him, and had him tied to a large pole in the middle of the small training pen. I had to pull over and watch as this beautiful black horse worked to preserve his independence under ropes and force. His body moved with strength and grace, and it was like watching an athlete do ballet. I made a mental note to check back on that horse one day, because something was really special about him.

The next time I went to visit no one was around, just this mysterious, beautiful horse. He came to greet me without hesitation, although he did not freely let me know him. It was then I realized he was a stallion, and that explained that energy that I could feel and see across the pasture. I stood for a long while, not attempting to touch him, only to let him smell me and feel my intention. I began to stop more frequently, and every time we knew each other more.

Several weeks ago I went there and saw the hired hands feeding the other horses. I motioned to them that I wanted to speak to them. I was beginning to fear that someone would report this crazy horse stalker and I would get in some kind of trouble, so I wanted their blessings regarding my new equine visitation therapy. The ranch manager said, "We know you and so does the horse, we see him come to you." I wanted to know more about him, and they told me he came from Mexico and they used him in the rodeos.

Well, I could see him in that role, as he had so much chutzpah and spirit. They told me I could come and visit anytime and it was okay by them if I fed him an occasional carrot or apple.

Now that I had their permission I came more often, and he came to the fence faster and faster. I do not even know what the draw is, but it is real and it is strong. I am certain that I am much softer and kinder than what he is used to, and I am sure he has a curiosity about the red headed woman who comes in the gold mini van. Last night I even went to see him in the dark, because I needed to. I wondered if he could see me in the pitch black, but he was at the fence before I was.

There is something about the simple act of visiting him that calms me, turns chaos into order, and fear into strength. When we are face to face and I ask him for nothing other than his presence, it is a rare and perfect gift.

The older I get the more I understand that old saying, "Come sit for a spell." Beauty, as I call him, gives me a reason to pause. I just want to sit next to him while the cars speed by and be grateful that I am sitting still, if only for a moment.

I think about the day I go there and he is gone; it makes me get a lump in my throat. Well, like all love affairs they come to an end, one way or another. But until our time is up I will treasure every moment I get to sit with him. I had horses much of my life, but this horse has me.

PART III. RELATIONSHIPS

Chapter Eleven

A Daily Cup of Waves

There could be no loss without first having love. To have loved is to have allowed an imprint on one's heart and soul forever more.

To sit with the ache of the void is to remember. Every cell in our bodies has been infused with the good memories, and it is in the remembering that the love comes up.

Even years after a person or pet has left us there will be days when, from somewhere down deep, a rush of feelings will come up and through us like a wave.

Do not run from it. Stand with your feet firmly planted in the moment and let it wash over you because truly it is not sadness, but rather love. It collects from all places stored in us and rushes to express itself without hesitation or preparation. It just is. So when that feeling comes, welcome it. It is love coming to visit.

Chapter Twelve

A Daily Cup of Passion

After all the years of defending passion for the sake of passion, I am finally understanding how destructive it can also be. I have read about how attachment to passion is to be curbed, and I thought the writer must certainly be as exciting as dry toast. Those writers must be devoid of that fire that is so fun to be burned by; that amazing, captivating, and all-encompassing passion of new love. Maybe this is on my mind because it is nearly Spring and I feel like I am coming out of seasonal and emotional hibernation? There is a new energy, a shift, a feeling of wanting to run barefoot through a meadow while the man of my dreams chases me. I imagine this will pass by June, but for now I am drawing deep breaths and contemplating new adventures with a new attitude.

Can a relationship exist without passion? Can it last? These are the questions that will always be asked. They are timeless, just like passion. Is it purely chemical and will it always fade? For me, it looks differently now.

Passion is now not just physical or chemical; it is soulful. It is about being heard, understood and maybe even affirmed. Hey, it could happen. Passion is great but intimacy is better. Intimacy can continue to grow when the initial passion fades. I think passion is the force that pushes us towards each other and intimacy is the glue that keeps us there. Intimacy can be created anytime two people exchange feelings and when those feelings are honored. These feelings do not even have to be agreed on, just heard.

Anytime two people can come together in the spirit of mutual respect to hear the other, there is an opportunity to create an even deeper connection. This is a learned skill and one that many people don't have. They are so filled with ego, defensiveness, and fear that they cannot be an open channel. This is not their fault; they are just not capable. My mistake has been trying to change other people instead of making better decisions and changing myself.

This morning it came to me that as long as I stay attached to the passion, how it takes me away from *me*, how it feels so good to be captivated and swept away, then the passion is in control and will continually have to be replicated. I hate reading about becoming disciplined about passion. I guess I have taken offense because I need/needed the lesson. Any time we are attached to something that has to be continually replaced, other than food, water, and shelter, then we are indebted to that feeling. This is true of being chemically altered in any way, including that new passion that puts the sizzle in our veins. Believe me, no one hates having to look at this more than I do, but it is a part of my story that has to be healed.

At Greek funerals they do not speak of achievements of the deceased but of their level of passion. This kind of passion is not to be confused with the kind of passion that consumes us in the beginning of relationships.

I cannot live without passion. Passion for the people I love, the way the air feels in the Spring, the way the rain sounds right now on my roof, the way a baby smiles at you, the way the sun shines through fall leaves, the way my first cup of coffee tastes, or the way I feel when I see an old couple walking and still holding hands. I am passionate about all of that, which is not to be confused with that new crazy love passion that always seems to fade. We can all only hope that when our biology regains its composure and we land on our feet, that intimacy replaces that original fire.

Although all fires go out eventually except for the Olympic torch, that what we hope we have left is a warm fireplace to sit around while holding hands and sharing our deepest fears and aspirations with the same person we originally fell in love with.

My God, what is happening to me? I feel like Danielle Steel, and I think hear the theme to "Love Story" in my head. I think I better go clean the garage now.

Chapter Thirteen

A Daily Cup of Projection

Today there seem to be a lot of people around me asking questions. They are the questions that at some point in your life you must ask if you are on the path. The answers to these questions are in the mirror and have just been waiting for you.

I have been divorced nearly nine years now. I thought for sure I would find my next prince and I would finish living the rest of my life with him in wedded bliss. Well, I guess Prince Charming fell off his horse on the way to my house, because that has not happened. There have been some loves, some I even thought I would spend my life with, but that did not come to pass.

The one thing I have learned in my time alone is how when there is another person around, it sure is easy to toss your unresolved issues all over them and then somehow make it look like their fault. I am now developing the very things that used to make me crazy about my ex-husband. When you are the only one that uses the walk-in closet, the "Whose side is cleaner?" game ceases to be fun. Now both sides are mine and they are a mess. I used to go nuts when my ex carelessly left his ATM slips around the car and house while I proudly kept track of mine and would methodically check them off in my checkbook. I barely even take them from the ATM machine now. I have a slight intention to deduct them, but I don't. There is no longer someone to be better than now, only me doing what I do, exactly the way I want to.

Now I see projection in the way I relate to my kids. I will often go into my son's room and scold him for his lack of organization, then go into mine and see that I have not unpacked my suitcase since last summer. There are half read books all over my floor and clothes hanging all over my inversion table that I never use. Not once have either of my children ever come into my room and told me it was a pigsty. So I am trying to be mindful of not expecting from them, or anyone, that which I do not do myself.

If I feel like my kids are being lazy, I will go for a walk. If I feel like someone is not treating me properly, I will treat myself with respect by speaking my truth. I am a sensitive woman, and it has been used against me my whole life. Sensitivity is good, right? I have come to learn that I can only feel hurt about something if I hold that belief within me somewhere.

I believe the more I rid myself of things that pinch me emotionally, the less I will need to use anyone else to relieve my own pain. When the pain is too much for us to accept and process, we often throw it to the ones we love the most, like a hot potato that lands in the innocent hands of the people closest to us. When I do this to my kids they know enough to say, "Mom, don't project your stuff onto us." I have taught them well, and although I am far from not doing this from time to time, we are all at least on the same playing field here in my home.

If I ever do marry again, I will bite my tongue about the many things that used to drive me crazy. It seems I used those experiences as some kind measuring stick to make myself feel bigger and better.

Anytime we are feeling superior or inferior, we are in some kind of fear. I will still always believe that I make coffee the best way, but even that I will just have let go of, and shut up and watch. And one day if I am lucky enough, perhaps he will bring me a cup in the morning along with a kiss, while I am getting ready in my half of the bathroom that will no longer be perfect. Sometimes I do not even put the lid back on the toothpaste, because hey, I just don't have to anymore.

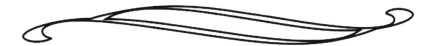

Chapter Fourteen

A Daily Cup of Why

I start my morning like I do most, checking my emails, deciding what is important enough to read or what I can tolerate emotionally. My finger hovers over the delete button as I scroll through all my messages. There are several from environmental, humanitarian, or animal rescue sites. It is with trepidation that I open and read most of these. That moment of hesitation before embarking on taking in what will surely make me *feel* is constant. Do I just ignore all the pleas for help from Haiti's children, the flood victims, American Humane Society's Second Chance Fund for abused animals, the rescue effort at the Gulf Coast, stopping Japanese whaling, the abused women of the world, the injustice of child labor, and human trafficking? The list goes on and on. With my first cup of coffee I sign petitions as well as share things I believe need to be exposed on my pages. Or I can also click delete and then go read a motivational book, and not let this darkness affect me.

However, it is almost with sadistic devotion that I force myself to read, learn, and hopefully make a small difference. Does the knowing change anything? It matters for me, because once you become awake it is hard to go back to sleep. I do wish I could pull life's covers over my head and go back into a land of unconscious slumber. However, you cannot heal what you do not know and the earth and all her inhabitants need to be healed. It is like watching a slow death between the air, oceans, soil, crops, climate, and the horrific things we perpetrate upon all living creatures.

I was prompted to write after reading success stories from the American Humane Society's Second Chance Fund for animals that have been rescued from deplorable and abusive situations. It is hard to read and watch the videos, but I do. I focus on the success stories of the animals that made it and the wonderful lives they now live. Millions of animals and humans are made to suffer at the hands of others. I go to a place in my brain to try to understand how another could inflict such abuse on another living creature, but come up empty handed every time. I cock my head to one side like a dog listening to new noise as I think it will help me find the answer, but it never does. The only thing that comes up is "Why?" A lack of love is all that makes sense. Surely someone who had been given adequate love and respect could not inflict such pain on another creature unless they were sociopathic or otherwise mentally ill. By extending love to others you are making a difference and that is something we can all do. By being compassionate with ourselves first we can then give it away. Often the problem just seems so huge that it feels like we are digging a hole in the sand and the hole fills in faster than we can dig.

I have had people tell me, "Kat, you cannot save the world." Well, I know this to be true, but I also know the person or animal that I choose to give love to is changed in that same world. Giving love really starts with how you give it to yourself. If you extend that which you have not truly mastered, then what you are giving is not authentic love but a way to mask your own pain. So, for today I will change the world by loving myself deeply, truly, and passionately. I will not speak an unkind word to my less than perfect parts; I will embrace all my light as well as the sharp edges. I will energize myself with that power that lifts me, and then I will go out into the world and give it away. I invite you to do the same.

PART IV. HOLIDAYS

Chapter Fifteen

A Daily Cup of Christmas Tradition

Christmas comes faster every year. It seems I have just put the last stray ornament away and then it is time to drag those boxes out all over again. It is with mixed emotion I do this, and I often question my resistance to the very thing that should be so joyful. I am by nature a nonconformist, so the act of doing what everyone else is doing goes against my grain. My neighbors add a new animated, brightly lit trinket every year, while I put up one less. I asked my kids, "What if every house that had lights took that money and fed the hungry or provided fresh water for someone on the planet instead of turning their house into job security for the power company?" I hate to be a killjoy, but this is the way my brain works.

We have had an artificial tree for about ten years now, and although I love the smell of the fresh cut pine in my home, I am somewhat pained to see this beautiful tree now dying for the sake of decoration. I have come to terms with this ritual by way of the same logic of the gifting of flowers. They are grown just for this purpose so it is not a waste, and the joy they bring is enormous. So I can justify it, but I have come to love my old fake tree that most likely came from China. It has become a part of the family and waits in the garage for its two weeks of glory every year.

My son Jon and I have the yearly job of assembling the stand. For the last three years it has been really challenging, as the holes where the screws go that brace it are all stripped. We now have figured out the basics and can put it together swiftly, but then we have to really tinker and Jimmy rig it to make it work.

Every year he grumbles about how the stand is junk and we need a new one, and every year I swear it will be the last time we use it. This year I asked him to go get the tree and have it in the house when I got home so we could assemble it after dinner.

Last year before I put everything away I wrote a note and tucked it into the stand, contemplating how many changes were going to take place in this next year with him now driving, and I wondered where we would be as mother and son a year from now? I also told him where I put the star, just in case I forgot or something happened to me. Sadly, this is the closest thing to a will that I have attempted. His dad used to hold him up to put the top of the tree on for the first five years, then he used a really high chair, then just a chair. Now he simply reaches right to the top and crowns our tree with one swift movement. When I see this, it makes me cry because it is a visual fact that he is not my baby anymore, and I am flooded with memories of his early, magical Christmases and how he used to tell Santa to "surprise me," instead of asking for anything.

This year the old, stripped, rickety metal tree holder was clearly not functional anymore. We sat for an hour, trying different ways to make it work. Being my father's daughter, and having been raised on a steady diet of determination and duct tape, I went and retrieved this silver magic that I have witnessed fix anything. I tightly wrapped it around the trunk, or piece of metal as it were, and then like a May Pole stretched it down and firmly affixed it to the bottom of the stand. I did this all the way around, much like tightening lug nuts on a wheel, and felt confident that our tree would remain erect one more year. Jon told me it looked "ghetto," which is one of his new favorite sayings. I told him, "It was the Velveteen Rabbit of trees; nothing a little tree skirt would not fix."

Emma, my 11-year-old, was anxiously awaiting her tradition, which is to put the first ornament on, but she had to wait until this ordeal was over with Jon and me. During this time, she got creative without us and decorated a ficus tree in the entryway. It looks Sunset Magazine worthy. I swear she is related to Martha Stewart. For as much resistance as I have, she has double the enthusiasm for this whole decorating ritual. She gave her tree a theme, and oddly it is the one I have always wanted to create on the family tree. I love the opalescent and purple ornaments, and have had a vision of having an artsy tree with coordinating colors that are soothing to the eye for many years. However, the children will never allow this, so every year we have an assortment of lovely ornaments; the ones that they made in preschool out of Popsicle sticks with their pictures inside, reindeer made out of corks and toothpicks, and some others that honestly I do not even recognize as they sit in the bottom of the box like dismembered parts of Santa's workshop. Every year I come close to throwing them away but I never do, and never will. My kids will have to dispose of them when I am long gone. Sorry, kids.

Both kids refuse to give up their old stockings. Emma's stocking still says, "Baby's First Christmas," and her name in glitter is peeling off. Jon's has a baseball-playing bear on it. I bought beautiful matching stockings for all of us many years ago, but they would have none of it. I love this about my children. Despite having an option for a bigger stocking, henceforth more goodies, they will stand firm in their tradition.

This year when we (who am I kidding, me) take Christmas down and put it away, I wonder if I will really throw away that stand that is now adorned with duct tape, as though it were branded with my family crest? The thought of having a base that works perfectly next year and all that we would have to do is put the tree in without incident makes me shudder. Despite this yearly frustration, it is one guaranteed hour of quality time with my son. It is just he and I, working as a team on this pathetic stand, down on the carpet with the dogs in our faces trying to help, while Emma flits around the house like a sugar plum fairy in her bliss. There are not many things that I get to do with my now almost 17-year-old son and this has become a yearly tradition that I look forward to. Maybe next year we will do it differently? He will be one month shy of 18, and however we do it, I just hope it takes us at least an hour and involves some communication and negotiating skills.

Maybe I will buy a new one and lose a few parts, just so we can figure it out together? Maybe I will even let him play Paul Bunyan and go cut one down, and together we drag it back to my minivan like we have bagged a deer? Yeah, maybe we should do that once? If we are going to get a real tree, we should be the ones to kill it, not get a factory farmed one. Oh, here I go confusing my causes again.

Happy holidays to all of you, and I hope you have something broken around your house so you too get to spend some quality time with the family fixing it. By the way, you can get duct tape at the Dollar Store. For me, that quality time has been the greatest gift of all.

Chapter Sixteen

A Daily Cup of Reindeer

People always ask me, "Where do you get your material?"

I always tell them the same thing.

"I just wake up and start my day, the rest always comes."

Now it appears that perhaps I attract more chaos than the average person, whatever that is, but I think it is God making sure I have lots to write about.

So let me share my morning with you. It is beautiful today, too beautiful for December in the Sierras, probably global warming. But I try to put that aside while I enjoy doing some yard work that I should have done in July. I am pruning my honeysuckle and grab a big, thick stem and snip it. I feel a sense of power and control having severed the biggest, fattest part of the vine. Well, I am happy to report that if that "stem" had been plugged in, I would not be here writing this.

You see, nestled in that little garden I have an electric reindeer with lights that moves its head. I did not want to use a white extension cord that would show, so I used a brown one to camouflage the fact that it was an electric reindeer. You never know who you might fool this time of year. It also occurs to me that despite my resistance I guess it is time to start wearing my glasses more often. I just never thought I would need them in the garden.

This year I am going to take my Christmas pictures that are on a CD (not because I have a digital camera, but because my friend insisted I use hers) to the store to try to figure out how to even see the damn pictures. I went yesterday and there were too many people with the same problem, blank stares on their faces, waiting in line for help. I finally gave up. I think I will just take my disposable camera that I bought to take the Christmas pictures in the first place, take pictures of the CD and send it out, saying, "Merry Christmas! My pictures are in here and I can't get them out!"

Chapter Seventeen

A Daily Cup of Christmas Expectations

As I placed my few simple decorations on my porch, I heard what sounded like a carnival up the street. I went to investigate and was met with bright lights, music, snowmen, penguins, elves, and an inflated Santa complete with all his reindeer. I was surprised there was not a brown out in the neighborhood. Ah, it is that time again, Christmas, and all the expectations that go into it. When I was a newly single mom I had to decide whether I wanted to buy the few gifts I could, or if wanted to buy decorations and make my house look like the Griswolds. I chose to spend my money elsewhere even though the kids begged for animation on the front lawn.

Then there are those Christmas cards to worry about too. Instead of spending money on a family card with pictures and writing a letter about how proud I am of my kids, even if they did not make the team or get straight A's, then spend money on postage to mail them only to have people toss them after saying, "Hey, look how big those kids are now," we did something different.

The kids and I made one big hand painted card of our beautiful mountains and decorated it. In our best glitter glue we wrote "Peace on Earth." Then we went to our friends' homes with homemade cookies and sang a Christmas carol while holding up our giant, hand-made Christmas card. Our traveling card was a tradition for many years, and one of the best memories I have of Christmas. It was the simplest of times; it was the best of times.

Let go of expectations this season and know that what really matters is being connected to those you love. It is not about keeping up with the Joneses; it is about being present, not giving presents.

Chapter Eighteen
A Daily Cup of Really Good Coffee

Every year my ex-husband buys me the same thing at Christmas. It's a bag of Peter James Coffee. He has had this delivered to his home every month for the last eight years. This coffee is so good, and I really appreciate the gesture. Coffee is a good gift for the mother of your children, especially when she is the one raising them 99.9% of the time. So for at least one month of the year I know I will have really great coffee to look forward to in the morning. God knows I need it. After the last bean is ground I know I will go back to whatever brand I may have been using before this extremely aromatic, oily, rich, robust, sensual coffee that graces my cupboard once a year. I feel like a princess every time I open the bag. This ritual serves as a nice gesture from a man, who used to be my husband, but it also brings up in me a certain sense of deprivation. I envy him for being able to afford this hand-delivered nectar of the Gods, and feel sad when my stash is gone. I feel like the Cinderella of coffee, and when the last cup is ritually consumed, "poof" I turn back into the brand X fairy. I realize this yearly ritual brings up my lack of abundance as well as my gratitude.

This year I think I will call this coffee company and see how much it would actually cost to have my very own delivered, just like him. Maybe I really can afford it? However, next year at Christmas it would take the excitement away when I received his offering. Maybe I can ask him for a maid, chauffeur, tutor, cook, coach, pet sitter, and gardener instead? Somehow, I think I would still get the bag of coffee, and for that I am grateful.

PART V. LIFE & DEATH

Chapter Nineteen

A Daily Cup of Dragonflies

Crickets sing, but no one knows why or what they are saying, they just sing. Things end up far away from where we start, and we don't get to know the answer to that either. Perhaps a day will come when I will understand the language of the universe.

The lacy veil of a dragonfly wing, so delicate and yet so strong all at once, carries it to places unknown. It is not afraid, it just goes there with ease. It does not know how fragile it is, it only knows it can fly.

The full moon is over all of us at once; everyone thinking it is just for them. However, it is a gift for all of us at exactly the same moment all over the planet. It is there to remind us how small we really are and that if we all looked up at once we would all be one. The stars are so far but their brilliance fills my heart, especially when under a blanket of stars in the desert.

The corners of myself not yet visited have been touched in loving you. I felt most like myself when I was extending my heart to you, and I now realize it was because I was loving myself right along with you. It was a different kind of love. I was more able to embrace things that were unlike me, but I loved you all the same.

You, like the dragonfly's wing, so fragile and yet strong all at once; carrying you to places unknown. I will not look back on this time with despair, but celebrate it as my awakening, my welcoming to myself.

Each moment is fleeting, impermanent, and one of a kind, and they all lead us to our brilliance. They all lead us home. I will see you again someday, as we are not complete. I may not know you, but I will recognize the way I felt with you, and when I touch you, I will remember.

Chapter Twenty

A Daily Cup of Contemplation

I have noticed that when it is time for me to learn something new, things come in threes. Things I had never heard of are now a part of my everyday reality, just like that! One day I am in judgment about someone else doing what I perceive to be silly or wrong, and the next thing you know I am doing that same thing.

This is especially true in parenting. Until you have raised your own kids, don't frown upon the mother losing it at the store. It is so easy to look saintly when you don't have kids in tow. Judgment is usually a way to stay insulated from the unknown or from what we fear.

Now, do I judge murder and violence as a bad thing? Yes, I certainly do, but I am referring more to our judgments about the behaviors and choices of others. I am currently in a spiritual re-birthing process and am letting go of many beliefs I have held fast. I experience the discomfort of not knowing exactly where I fit, or if I even have to fit. I choose to believe that what a person needs to hold onto at that time in their lives is exactly where they need to be. For now I am open, so open it scares me a bit, as there is no boundary to hold me. My current mantra is, "I only know one thing for sure, and that is that I don't know anything except that I believe in everything and nothing."

Far be it from me to tell *you* how to believe or where you will go after you die. If I had died and come back, well I would then be on a soapbox, but that is not my reality.

111

I have my own personal beliefs, but my job is not to try to convince you to be just like me. It is my job to honor what you need to do, that which makes you inherently you. I think we are a frightened lot, and to stand alone in your beliefs without a trail of people in front of or behind you is most challenging. I often visualize all the man-made religions split into two groups facing each other, while giving their best sales pitch as to why they are the chosen ones and everyone else is wrong. This would be a long line and the visual in and of itself always amuses me.

I know for myself that what I perceive to be the energy that makes the planet spin, gives the rose its fragrance, a baby its first smile, the light in a creature's eyes when you hold their gaze, the way you feel when someone tells you they love you and mean it, the oneness we feel in a disaster, the way a sunset is never the same and most of all, the way it feels to be honest and vulnerable with another person, is a power greater than myself that I believe connects us.

All I really know is that there is a force so strong, so magnificent and loving, that when I am open enough to radiate and receive it I know I am tapped into something far greater than any man-made manufactured belief system. It is, I am. Now is the time in my life when I am turning like a lake, the bottom goes to the top, and all things that don't serve me are sorted out and removed. I love these times and I feel them coming like the scent before a rain. I am also fully aware that there may be lots of rain, thunder and lightning, but I also know what comes at the end. To see a rainbow is the greatest sign there is that the darkness has ended and the light has been restored. I am getting my umbrella and a lawn chair and making myself ready for the show.

Chapter Twenty-One
A Daily Cup of White Mice

When my mother came home to my house to make her transition in January 2009, I allowed my daughter to purchase two white mice. I can still hear her now, "But Mommy, they only cost two dollars." I had vowed not to have any more animals in cages, but with all the time I was spending care taking my mother, I thought it would be a good thing for her to have something to nurture as well. I lost my beloved dog of nearly 16 years three weeks before my Mom came to my house, so we were all very sad about that too. Charlotte and Mariline came home to live in my daughter's room. This gave her something to take care of while I was giving care to my Mom. Emma and the mice were really sweet together.

Charlotte, the bigger and sweeter mouse, was the one we played with the most because she was tamer. She would just close her eyes when you would stroke her head, and was content to sit in your lap.

A few days after we got the mice my Aunt Peggy arrived to say goodbye to her sister. She stayed in my daughter's room along with the mice. One morning I just happened to get up very early and there stood my Aunt with her pajama top folded up, cradling one of these mice. She had gotten up to go to the bathroom and the mouse had squeezed out of the cage and our cat was right there, just seconds away from a morning snack. Her face was frozen, and I knew she was scared to death as she moved slowly towards me to deposit her in my hands.

Had she not awakened early it would have been a tragic ending and a tearful morning. I think the mouse she saved was Mariline but I cannot be sure as we only had them a day or two. My Aunt was an angel that morning for that mouse.

My Mom passed later that week on January 25th, and I will never be the same after helping her to the other side. She brought me into the world and I helped her out of this one. It was a full and complete circle of love and life.

After all the family went home we finished the last of the casseroles, and we grieved and celebrated and grieved some more. Life went on as it always does and will, and we grew more fond of these mice, taking them out as often as we could. Charlotte got very sick with cancer about five months ago and we took her to the vet to end her suffering. The entire staff was in tears as were we. My poor daughter loved this little pet so much but there was nothing we could do. We buried her on her little pink mouse bed in the garden with a dozen other pets that have passed before her. Now only Mariline was left. She was a bit wild and ran in circles with grief after her sister died. We now handled her more and in time she mellowed and turned into a completely different mouse. We thought about getting a new one to keep her company, but then there would always be one left and sometimes they don't accept a new mouse. So we decided to give her all the love we had as an only child mouse.

Six weeks ago my Aunt Peggy, the only child left in her family, passed away on April 15th and it was a bit of a shock. I never thought I would lose her so soon after my mother. I got to say my goodbyes over the phone and promised her I would stay in touch with her kids. She told me over and over again while she stayed with me that this was a great worry for her, having to leave her kids behind. She was troubled being the only one left in her family of origin and said, "I am an orphan now." She passed peacefully and I am now coming to terms with her absence as well. The remaining mouse, Mariline, became ill about a month ago and off we went to the vet yet again. The two-dollar mice are now worth two hundred dollars. People thought I was crazy taking mice to the vet, but they were a part of our family and we loved them as much as the dogs and cats. They didn't really know what was wrong with her but gave me some medication in hopes that it would help her ears. Well, her ears never got better and after I started using this medication she seemed much worse in other ways, too. It may have just been a coincidence but she went downhill from there. I have looked in on her every morning for a month thinking she would be gone, but she crawled into my hand like every other day. In these last few weeks I have held her in my lap while I type, and have rubbed the side of her face with regularity while she would close her eyes and bring her little paw up to her face in a state of bliss. Every day we would repeat this ritual and she would chatter at me, and I knew she was happy and felt safe. The joy of being able to provide comfort to this tiny creature was huge for me. I knew it would not last and warned myself about how it was going to feel when she was gone, but I chose to continue the ritual. I knew that every day I gave her love and comfort I was giving it to myself as well.

That is how love is . . . you cannot keep it from yourself when you give it away. Today I took her outside. It was nice and I wanted her to feel the sun for a bit and get some fresh air. I held her on my lap for a short time while I rubbed her back, feeling her little backbone where there once was fat. I brought her cage out so she could be out in the backyard with me while I watered. My fear was that she would die alone and I would come home and find her, but it did not happen that way. I saw her on her side in the cage and ran over to scoop her up. She was leaving, and I wanted to hold her while she went. I cupped her in my hands, just holding space for her while she left. She took her last little breath and that was that. The light was gone that had been in her eyes just a second before. And like my mother, I now did not recognize this little creature. She was just a body, devoid of the spark that gave her the personality and love she had. I cried and at the same time was relieved for her. Her breathing had been labored for weeks, and I could not believe she hung on so long. I think she hung on because she knew I would be coming for her every day like I had been for weeks, to hold her in my lap in the little blue blanket while I worked on the computer.

So sixteen months later, my dog BJ, my mother Ruth, Charlotte, Aunt Peggy, and Mariline are all gone. Each loss invokes the memories of the loss before. I went back outside to feel the sun and the cool water on my feet and listen to the birds. I had this rush of "Never again, don't do it ever again, Kat. Don't put yourself out there, protect yourself from the pain of loss. No more animals, no more loves. That is the safer, saner way to be in this world. The pain of losing the things you love is just not worth it."

Just then a yellow finch came out of nowhere and flew in a perfect circle above my head. My mother sent ten finches to the tree outside my window the day after she passed. I asked her if she could swing it to let me know she made it to the other side okay before she died, and I am quite certain they were her gift to me. I don't ever have more than one finch in my yard, and certainly not in the dead of winter. The finches came all week after she died, until the side of my house looked like an aviary. A year to the date later the finches came back to the same tree and I smiled, knowing full well there was a magical power at work far bigger than I could ever imagine. I know with love comes loss, that you cannot have one without the other. I guess if I had to shed tears and feel the pain of losing the people and things I love, truly it is a small price to pay for the gifts that love brings. We all have that spark and I don't know where it goes, but it does not die. Nothing is permanent but change, and with great love comes great loss. Even if you spend your entire life with the person you love, you ultimately will have to say goodbye.

Chapter Twenty-Two
A Daily Cup of L'Air Du Temps

My mother was not fussy about her appearance. She was a natural beauty with raven hair and a waist like Natalie Wood. I remember the way her elegant fingers looked when they played "Green Sleeves" on the piano. There was an audible click her nails made on the keys while she caressed them and coaxed them into music. I did not feel like my mother, but more like my father. I both envied and hated the way she did womanhood. She was a beauty, I was an athlete. She depended on my Dad for everything, I depended on no one, as I clearly saw what happened when you invested too much in a man. She couldn't put gas in her car, while I could change my oil. She waited for him to come home, while I ran away from it.

There were a few things that she purchased to celebrate her femininity. She rarely wore make-up and never had her nails done, as they were just naturally beautiful. I made some once out of clay, but they weren't like hers. They melted off the tips of my fingers like the wicked witch in the *Wizard of Oz*. I did not feel like "my little pretty," but rather a wannabe.

Next to her bathroom sink there sat a bottle of L'Air du Temps. I don't know what it even means in French, but the way my mother said it made it sound exquisite. I believe there was a little bird made of frosted glass on the top. I really don't remember smelling it on her but I am sure my Dad did and that was who counted.

When I participated in the eWomen Network's international talent contest in Dallas in 2009 I really wanted my Mom to be with me in some way. I put some of her perfume on some cotton balls in a zip lock bag to take with me, along with her picture and a candle. I made a little altar in my hotel room before I left to take on the show of my lifetime. I spent time connecting with my Mom, asking her to be with me. I had the honor of helping her pass just six months before that in my home and it changed me forever. I won that contest with a perfect score of three 10's and there was no doubt my mom was right there with me; she was my biggest fan.

One should always use the fancy bottle of perfume along with the good dishes and crystal, because one day you will leave it all behind. A far better use of the perfume would have been to be on her skin rather than sitting on my bathroom vanity, reminding me of her daily. I just put some on and memories of my mother swirled in and around me, so I guess I am glad there was still a little left.

I wish she were still here to say "L'Air du Temps" out loud to me. She spoke French, and she said it so elegantly that it would make it smell so much better

Chapter Twenty-Three

A Daily Cup of Letting Go of Laughter

It has been two weeks today since I got the text that Robin Williams died. I stared in disbelief at my phone when my son texted me. I thought certainly it was a hoax, the same kind that promises me I will make a dollar from Bill Gates every time I share a message on Facebook. The reality finally seeped into all my conscious crevices like a cold rain.

The year I started comedy I watched Robin Williams dazzle a sold-out crowd at the Metropolitan Opera House and I wept. I thought, "What would it feel like to have that many people love you like that?" I do so hope he really knew the answer to that.

The marriage between despair and humor seems inseparable. Laughter and tears have the same cord that connects them on opposite ends. Perhaps the funniest person in the room might also just be the loneliest? After the lights go off and the audience and help goes home, there you are all alone. I have stood on stages with thousands of people in front of me and then gone back out in the dark to feel what that felt like too. It is like looking at the Thanksgiving dishes when everyone has gone home. One minute there is all this energy and admiration for you, then poof; the lights go out and that moment of deep connection with the audience is broken. It is gone as fast as the neon lights fade. Then you are eating a to-go meal on a white towel on your hotel room bed, watching late night television.

I have been a comic for 27 years and in the last few years I have heard another voice inside my head, or maybe it is in my heart? The need to touch and inspire people has become as great as wanting to hear the laughter. When you are a stand up comic you are a professional people pleaser. If comics tell you they don't care if the audience liked them, they are lying. We are in the business of getting you to love us. Is there ever enough of that love? Is there enough to erase away whatever pain makes us stand up in front of strangers and work for approval and a paycheck? We are as good as our last set, and until we can rectify a bad one we carry that memory with us until we have erased it with laughter. Then we are redeemed once again. I have lots more to share than jokes, and really at my core is my story. A story of feeling different and out of place, but in the laughter I felt at home. The more I know and accept myself the less I need that approval.

Three years ago I made a conscious decision to start acting on my deepest dream, which was to not just do comedy but also be an inspirational speaker. The first few times I spoke from my heart without punch lines I had to really stay centered and know that just because they were not laughing did not mean they were not listening and *feeling*. Jokes are immediate gratification, while touching people at their core is usually done in complete silence. I panicked the first few times because I was so accustomed to the laughter and applause. I had to trade what I could not hear for what I could *feel*. I could sense souls being moved, I could see the tears in their eyes, and I knew in those moments of complete silence that I was making a difference. I knew my story, challenges, and authenticity were moving people. I knew that my honesty was allowing them to speak their truth too. This new connection was deep and gratifying. I will always make people laugh and comedy will always be a part of who I am, but the sacred silence will now mean as much to me as the laughter.

PART VI. AWAKENINGS

Chapter Twenty-Four

A Daily Cup of Perfection

As I was attempting to get my van windows clean this morning, it was hard to differentiate which spots were on the inside and which were on the outside. As I continued in this pursuit of perfection it occurred to me that was also how we see the world and those in it. We can only see through our own spots, streaks, stories, and wounds. When something really bothers you about someone, there is good information in there. I have long hated that saying, "If you spot it you got it," and my ego will try to analyze that away. This is not to say when I see horrific acts of cruelty and violence that I am like that to others, but have I ever been that way to myself? Yes, I have been less than loving to myself at times. I am referring more so to when we have an ongoing annoyance with someone. Do we own a bit of the same story? For instance, when my daughter comes home from school, I often ask her right away to do her chores. I see used drinking glasses and plates in her room and it irritates me to no end. Do I have coffee cups and left over plates in my office sometimes? I absolutely do. This attempt to rectify behavior in others when we in fact have the same behavior seems to have gone on since the earth's crust cooled. We have long tried to get others to see it our way, and that dance will continue until the sun burns out. My daughter taught me a great lesson when she was about three years old. I picked out an adorable outfit for her but was met with great resistance. I was in disbelief. I mean, how could any little girl not think this was a precious outfit?

After several failed attempts at convincing her to put it on, she placed her hands on her tiny hips and looked up at me with complete conviction and said, "Mommy, everybody has their own certain ways." No truer words were ever spoken. I will spend more time trying to clean my own metaphoric windshield so that I might see less imperfection in others. Now, where is that mental microfiber cloth?

Chapter Twenty-Five

A Daily Cup of Ego

I cannot get away from ego. It lives in me, as well as in you. I am told it is there for survival, so if I were being chased by a saber-toothed tiger I would be grateful for its presence. I have not seen a tiger lately but my ego visits daily. They say there is a certain price for awareness and I think my yearly installment is due. I am aware enough to know I am in my ego, but not evolved enough to silence it. In fact the more I try to ignore it the more it screams, stamps its feet, and jumps up and down. It is like that ill-behaved child in the grocery store that does not get its way, and you judge the kid as spoiled and the parent as weak. And then you go on to birth one exactly like that. I know for a fact that anytime I try to control something outside of myself I am in my ego. However, my ego is "in" me, so does that still apply? The ego is like a big squeaky part in my head, and the old saying "the squeaky wheel gets the grease" certainly applies here, so it gets my attention. I am able to observe myself as the thinker, which places me just outside the ring of fire but still close enough to get burned. My days have become a mental abacus of "oh, there it is again, you are in your ego." I now wonder if that is my ego gratifying itself by keeping track, like the snake that eats itself without even realizing it? I cannot find a simple answer to this painful dilemma.

I know there is an answer, as I know people who have mastered this. I know they would say, "You are on the path because you realize that it is happening, and that is the first step." It kind of feels like someone has given me a key to a new car, but it will not open it. Since there is no quick fix here, I guess I just keep retooling the key, grinding off the rough spots that prevent me from opening the door. I just get to sit in the awareness of not being there yet, but live with the belief that one day I will be.

Who am I without my ego? I am you.

Chapter Twenty-Six

A Daily Cup of Fortune Cookies

You know you do it. I do it, we all do it. At the end of that usually way too oily Chinese dinner we get that sealed fortune cookie on the brown tray with the bill we cannot read. Even if you don't like the fortune cookie, you know you look forward to cracking it open to find that message along with your lucky red lotto numbers on the back. I wonder if anyone ever goes to the casino with that little slip of paper, in search of their fortune? We all read them aloud to each other and secretly hope that ours is the right one for us. If it is not, we just assume they grabbed ours first but it was really meant for us. I have even saved them in my wallet until they disintegrate into lucky dust.

I had dinner with a man recently who was most self-centered and only spoke about himself. When he cracked open his fortune cookie it was empty. I had to laugh and told him maybe it was a sign? I also then acted co-dependently and gave him mine. I am fascinated by how much stock we put in these dry little folded cookies that are made out of God knows what?

If we are that impressionable about what this bit of hope predicts, then why don't we do that every day? Why save this little custom for Chinese dessert? Why not keep a jar in your home and every day pick one out before you leave? These cookies could be filled with inspiration and encourage kindness for yourself and the planet.

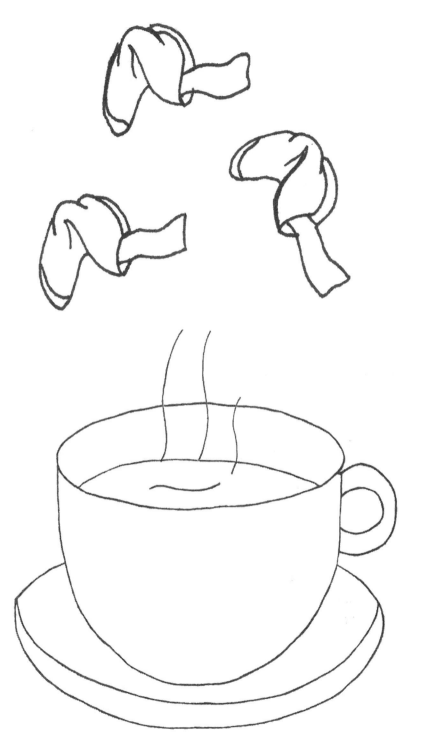

If we are so easily coached and motivated by a cookie, it would be great if we could use these little treats more often for a higher purpose. That being said, if I could give you all a fortune cookie it would say, "If all you ever do is become the best version of yourself that you can be, then you have succeeded." By the way, I recommend #28, tofu with veggies.

Chapter Twenty-Seven

A Daily Cup of Toilets

I think when the plumber worked on this house he planted a microchip in both toilets that would make them malfunction on exactly the same day. How is that mathematically even possible?

As of last night both toilets won't stop running. I jiggled and wiggled the handle, I took the tank lid off and put my hand down into that cold and hopefully e-coli free water. You know it is separate water, but you always wonder. Like reaching into the garbage disposal knowing full well it is off but wonder if somehow it will magically turn on with your hand down there. I lifted the bobble, I pressed down on the gasket, and I stretched the chain, only to now hear the continual flow of water through my toilet.

I am really conservative and don't waste anything. This really gets my obsessive side triggered, so I manually turn off the water to both toilets. Success at last, at least for the moment. I feel like a pioneer woman of sorts. We will just have to turn on the water in the outhouse when we need it. As I bend over to turn the water back on this morning, after the whole family had used the bathroom, I realize I really do not want to be this personally involved with my toilet and realize a call to the plumber is imminent. I know how expensive this will be and think there must be a way to do it myself. Then I remember the near electrocution of working in the garden a few days ago, and think that I am really not up to flooding the house just before the holidays. Okay, where is that number?

Chapter Twenty-Eight

A Daily Cup of Empathy

You know, inside each of us resides "the place." One cannot describe it really, it simply is. This place in me without a description calls out to the same place in you. It is magnified when recognized in others. It is that moment when you connect with others, feel their pain and their joy, and sense their feelings as though they were your own. It is in that empathy that we are all one. It is a rainbow of light that bridges our aloneness and speaks softly to that voice within that does not use words. It is love. It cannot be bought, seen or touched, but it is real and it is big. When "that place" does not get to exercise by way of giving and receiving, it calls out for attention. It feels empty or flat and wants to be alive with the vibration when connection is lacking. It is "that place" where words are not important and yet it says more than any book or saying we could ever read. It is "that place" where I acknowledge you at the deepest level, and it is the true experience of being human. This feeds "that place" and makes it and us stronger more connected people. To be a witness to another's pain or joy allows us to hold within us the magic of empathy, and without it there can be no real love. It allows us to be in another's shoes, to experience feelings that exist outside ourselves, to extend something to another when they are broken or filled with joy.

I honor that place in each and every one of you on this day, and know that I hold a sacred space in "the place" in me that connects with the same in you.

Chapter Twenty-Nine

A Daily Cup of Activism

In a world where people extrapolate what they want or need from the Bible, I believe the word "dominion" is one that is often skewed. I am not a scholar or theologian, but I do believe our creator would never have meant for us to oppress, torture, exploit and abuse animals in the way we do. Dominion does not mean, "Do with them whatever you want."

"Stewardship" is also mentioned, and we have been given the responsibility to take care of the earth and the animals. The animals are not here *for* us; they are here *with* us. I have had some conversations recently with people about judgment and not allowing one's energy to become ruffled in trying to be an advocate for the voiceless. I often hear from them, "I cannot change the world so I will just stay in a place of peace and not allow myself to be affected." Even if I tried, I could not be one of those people. I believe if you witness abuse and do nothing, then you are part of it. If you know better you do better, and so many people are not willing to look at the truth.

Tomorrow is Martin Luther King Jr. Day. I am grateful for the activists in this world who do not just sit back and keep their mouths shut and their energy nice and tidy. I applaud the people who speak up, step up, and take a risk to bring about change. To show up for those who cannot, whether they are human animals or belong to another species, is an integral part of our evolution.

Change is happening regarding animal abuse, inhumane conditions in factory farming, and cruel blood sports. Kill shelters are slowly being eradicated and communities are coming together to insure changes are implemented. These changes would not be happening if people stayed in denial and did not want to get their hands messy. I saw *Selma* the other day and expected long lines and a sold out theater because it's about Martin Luther King Jr., but there were just a handful of people in there. On the other hand, *American Sniper,* the real life story of Navy Seal Chris Kyle, was sold out show after show after show. Both true stories, one man changes the world through peace and the other with killing 160 terrorists and protecting countless marines. Both are heroes in my book, and no matter what your opinions are about civil rights or war, these two men stepped up and fought for what they believed in and paid the ultimate price.

Chapter Thirty

A Daily Cup of Seven Minutes

I have heard it said that for every cigarette you smoke, you take seven minutes off your life. I used to smoke many years ago, so I have added up the time in my head. I often wonder what I would do if I only had seven minutes left to live?

I might see one of my grandchildren being born or the most amazing double rainbow. I might get to give my son or daughter a hug before getting married or watch them open their Christmas presents one last time. I might enjoy a lazy Sunday morning with a cup of coffee while reading the paper or I could go for a walk with my dogs and wonder how they always act like it is first time they have been out. I could take one more bubble bath with candles while counting my blessings. I could smile at someone I don't know or hold a door open for an older person while their eyes twinkled a grateful "thank you." I could retrieve a ball from the street for a child and keep them safe from danger. I could sit with my best friend and look back over all the crazy things we've done and wonder why we were so lucky to still be here. I could go visit my parents and bring them a casserole, which would mean they could relax that night. I could brush my daughter's hair and tell her how beautiful she is from the inside out. I could take seven minutes of my time and share with someone how important it is to love themselves before it is too late. Because one day it will be, and you just never know what you could have done with seven more beautiful minutes.

BONUS CHAPTER

What is in your Daily Cup today?

I hope you enjoyed this book. As a bonus, I've included blank daily cups and pages so you can create your own drawings and write down your own thoughts and inspirations. Let my book become your book. This book started with one story and yours can too.

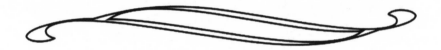

Acknowledgments

I would first like to thank my parents, Ruth and Ted Short, for gifting me with my life, sense of humor, and supporting my decision to become a comedian even if my dad's mantra was, "You need a career you can fall back on." Three decades later I think he trusts my decision. My mom was a writer but never got that book published, so I did this for you too, Mom. I still hear the sound your nails made on your typewriter.

To my children, the two best decisions I have ever made in my life. Jonathan and Emma Stamper, thank you for helping me grow up to be me and for showing me what unconditional love feels like. I love you more than mere words can express. The sound of your laughter has been the most beautiful thing I have heard in this lifetime. I hope you will always find reasons to laugh. This book was a labor of love for me and my daughter Emma, who at the young age of seventeen became my illustrator. This book is as much hers as mine, and I could not be more proud. She has amazed me with her artistic abilities and vision. I appreciate her contribution so very much. She is a very talented artist and I hope she will share her gifts and talents with the world.

Thank you to Sue Schrader and Judi Hertzog, my first mastermind partners. I am not sure I would have ever made the leap had it not been for you two. Your belief in me helped me get into the car and drive off to my dreams and new life that day, nearly thirty years ago.

To my uncle Zeke Fairchild, who tried to bribe me with a computer if I became a writer instead of a comic when I lived with him after I first arrived in Los Angeles. I explained that comedy was writing but he still wanted me to write a book, so here it is, Zeke. For my aunt Marilyn Short, who was always one of my biggest fans and encouraged me to write as well. I literally promised her in her final moments that I would write a book, and I always keep my promises.

Thanks to Lynn and Morris Walker, who saw me perform standup comedy the very first time in Lake Tahoe, and told me to never stop. They told me that I could be the next Carol Burnett if I wanted to and have been great supporters ever since.

To Lenny Bruce's mother, Sally Marr, who saw a tape of me, thought I was funny, and invited me to her home in Hollywood to discuss my career over egg salad sandwiches. Her belief meant the world to me even though I had no idea who she was when she first called me.

I had a home economics teacher at Wooster High School and her name was Alice Bauer. She later became Alice Vawter. I remember her asking me what I was going to do after I graduated? At that time in my life I could only see as far as my boyfriend's future. I told her I did not know if I would go to college or not. I wish I could recall her exact words forty years later but I cannot. I just remember how she made me feel. I think we were standing in front of a pristinely clean stovetop having this conversation. She encouraged me to explore who I was and to find my talents. She was insistent that I go on to study something after high school. Now my parents and grandparents had been planning my future for a long time, and I let it go in one ear and out the other. I really had no desire at that time continue with school. However, something she said flipped a switch in me, and I did in fact go on to get a BA in Social Services and Corrections at the University of Nevada Reno. Good teachers see their students and encourage them. I hope I can find her and give her a copy of this book because I am sure she has no idea how much her words meant to me. She also taught me how to make the perfect hard-boiled egg, and to this day, I hear her voice telling me just how to do that. So thank you Mrs. Vawter, wherever you are, you made a difference in my life.

Thanks to every person who has ever encouraged me to write. To anyone who ever came up to me after a show and thanked me and said, "You have *it*." I may not remember your names, but I remember your faces and how you made me feel, and I will never forget that.

In conclusion, I would not be writing this if it were not for my mentor and friend, motivational speaker Donna Hartley. She is the first person I ever met in show business. After a coaching session I mentioned I really needed to write that book. In a split second, she snatched up her phone and when the woman on the other end answered, she said, "Pam, I have a new client for you." I wanted to run screaming out of her house, "No, not now, I am not ready!" But it was too late. She handed the phone to me and that is how this book came to be. A million thanks to my editor Pam Vetter, who was on the other end of that phone call. Her patience, guidance, insight, and creative input have made a lifelong dream a reality. She has been a treasure to work with and deserves a medal and a week at a five star spa!

About the Author

Kat Simmons is a 30-year veteran of the international comedy club circuit. You may have seen her at The Improvs, Catch A Rising Star, or on the Comedy Channel, Fox's Comedy Tonight, or on Candid Camera. She won the eWomen Network's international talent contest in Dallas in 2009. She was a regular cast member in the touring comedy revue, "Boomerang," a baby boomer comedy bash.

Kat has a unique talent for combining physical comedy with real life situations that everyone can relate to. She has been favorably compared to the masters of the craft: Lucille Ball, Carol Burnett, and Red Skelton. She is one of a few physical comediennes working today. You may recognize yourself in some of her material as she honestly shares with the audience as though they were all longtime friends. She delights in bringing to the stage the very things most people keep a secret. She speaks the truth, making it easier for the rest of us to be honest with ourselves.

Kat has a versatility and approachability that makes her perfect for large corporate functions, casinos, comedy clubs, and private parties. She has a knack of incorporating the group at hand into her show and finding that common thread. She makes them part of her performance. She has performed for a wide variety of groups from tow truck drivers and fence contractors to doctors and engineers. She is a favorite at women's events because she tells it like it is. Her humor is clean and elevates and enlightens her audiences. As a result, she is a favorite at health and wellness seminars, medical associations, and the American Heart Association.

She has appeared with Tim Allen, Kevin Nealon, Kenny Rogers, and Rob Schneider. She had the honor of following legendary motivational speaker Zig Ziglar, after receiving his lifetime achievement award. She is not only a comedienne, but an inspirational humorist making her a great choice for your keynote speaker as well. She loves to share her own spark to help ignite yours.

Kat moved back from Los Angeles to the beautiful Carson Valley (just below Lake Tahoe) in 1992 to do what she loves in the area she loves. She came back to have her children, Jonathan and Emma. While not in the hub of Los Angeles, it provided her with new opportunities she would otherwise never had. She quickly began doing corporate events and she hosted and produced her own comedy show for 15 years at the Carson Valley Inn Casino in Minden, Nevada. She also has taught standup comedy workshops for the past eighteen years and it is her greatest joy to help others find their empowerment through humor. Kat says, "Comedy is not what I do, it is who I am."

www.KatSimmons.com

Facebook Kat-Simmons Entertainer

https://twitter.com/katsimmonscomic

https://www.instagram.com/katlaffs/

Made in the USA
Charleston, SC
23 August 2016